BUCKLES TIES LOOPS RINGS WRAPS AND CLASPS, BABY!

Maiche Lev

BUCKLES TIES LOOPS RINGS WRAPS AND CLASPS, BABY!

by Maiche Lev
All Rights Reserved
Copyright © 2021 HDW Publications

This book may not be reproduced, transmitted, or stored in whole or in part by any means, including graphic, electronic, or mechanical without the express written consent of the publisher except in the case of brief quotations embodied in critical articles and reviews.

Cover and book design by David Bricker

ISBN: 978-0-9975757-8-1

Contents

And Once 1
Y' Don't Say… 3
Common Needs 5
Mr. Augustus von Fürderfromm 7
A Closer Look 9
Bath Drain 11
My Hollywood Ladies 13
My Other Latest Smallest (Old Remote Controls) 17
Poor Girl 19
Strummer 23
Zion 25
These Poor People 27
I Was in Bed 29
On Top of Africa Hot 31
Maladjustment 33
Factoid 37
We Can't Do It 39
St. Vincent Beach 41
Fabio 43
Lucille 45
Love 47
Dylan Live 51
Genealogy 55
Nerdy 57
Dungeons and Dragons 59

Dear Me ... 61
If You Knew ... 63
Letter to a Long-term Junkie ... 67
Be Good to Someone ... 69
What You Never Forget ... 71
Meyer Boy (My Sister's Dog) ... 73
Chuck Mangione (pre-digital) ... 75
Smile ... 77
Marvin Gaye ... 79
Someday, Then and There ... 81
Crowd Roars ... 85
Smoking Crack with Dennis Miller on a Sunday Morning ... 87
Surprises ... 89
Just a Song Before I Go ... 93
The Life Within ... 95
Loving and Laughter ... 97
On Father's Day (with D. Bricker) ... 99
Good Sex ... 101
You're into Me Like… ... 103
Ha Eisha Sabra ... 105
Stalking is… ... 107
Find Your Way Back ... 111
Beware ... 113
Whistling a Tune ... 115
Gender Reassignment ... 117
A Voter ... 123
For Darren ... 125

Flip-Flops 131
One-Sided Thought on Modern-day Teen Rebellion 133
I ♥ 137
Gritty Corsage.. 141
Another One.. 143
More Later... 145
He Would Know…... 147
Bruce Jenner 149
People 151
Trump 153
Hypermasculine Horseshit Falls....................................... 155
There You Go 157
I'd Like to…... 159

For Darren

And Once

Once someone didn't call me back
And they woke up with fully-grown asparagus spears in their garden
And once...
Strange, fat, curly-tailed lizards invaded our county
And the slender, green, sinewy breed were no more
And once...
Huge buzzards called "turkey vultures" rode the thermals with their blacks wings against the sun
And you thought of the eagles on the Nazi officers' caps
And once there was a melaleuca tree
Which is native to a small strip of land between Poland and Upper Volta
Someone brought the seeds back in their ski boots
The melaleuca's so thirsty...
It drank up half the Everglades
And most of Lake Okeechobee
People said you could watch it grow!

And then a New York socialite womanizing glazed donut came to rule the land!
He tried to use expressive hand gestures but it didn't work at all for him
In fact, it was just plain peculiar
Foreign dignitaries did not know what to think

But more than anything
Every time this leader spoke
He used personal superlatives
Telling the people history surrounded him
Like confetti in an endless parade
He said "hell" a lot, too
He sucked royally
And more than half the people were really glad he was gone

Y' Don't Say…

I came in through the side door
'Cause the front door was locked
Came in through the window
'Cause the back door was blocked

Came in through the cellar
'Cause the loft was occupied
Came in through the vents
'Cause the chimney was full of flies

Came in by the doorbell
The mailbox was in the street
Came in through the rafters
'Cause the clothesline was pinned with sheets

I came in through the workroom
'Cause the ladder in the shed was rusted
I hid away in the gutters
'Cause the handyman was not to be trusted

Came in through the Florida room
'Cause the mosquito light was zappin'
Came in through the orchid blooms
'Cause the gas tank wasn't happenin'

COMMON NEEDS

Endgame politics are arrived at
When two partisans meet at that fork in the road
Where they do or do not treat each other fairly
Each with common needs

Endgame politics are arrived at
When two heads of state meet up
And do or do not treat each other fairly
Their citizenry all with open hands
Common needs

The only thing unanimous in endgame politics
Is that moment between war and peace
In which preeminence exercises its capacity to be humane …
   or not
The renegade spirit runs amok into the next generation's
   prejudice and grudge
And yes…
Common needs

Mr. Augustus von Fürderfromm

When I first arrived in Pensacola, I went to the Home Depot and bought twenty pounds of birdseed—the cardinal mix, I think—and I bought the usual stuff you get when you first move in: shelving, cleansers, a rake. (I held off on the wind chimes.)

The albino squirrel and his brown little friend play dive-bomber games with the bluebirds and their rookery mates, pecking and feeding.

The neighbor's tailless calico prowls like a bobcat along the inner cusp of the unpainted, untreated wood plank fence.

Someone on the lawn crew stole my SCUBA belt; I must have left it in plain view.

The two Texans—29 and 30—who had given me taxi rides for a month turned out to be junkies. They pawned my bicycle—an $1800 Fuji with dual suspension, an Excelsior with a ride soft enough to pad the fifth and sixth vertebrae in their titanium cage inside my neck. If they had house-sat another week, any appliance that fit through the door would have been sold, no doubt.

What would it be like to be a falconer?

Someday I'll own my own bowling ball.

East Hill. Someone tried to rob the convenience store. The proprietor shot the thief dead before he made his way out the door.

My neighbor across the street, a black man named Roy, has asked to borrow $140 so far this year. His girlfriend came hysterically knocking at 3:30 a.m. a few weeks back. I let her in.

Then he barged in after her, punched her, and kicked her while I tried to separate the two of them. Roy went to my kitchen, looking for a knife. Not finding one, the two of them left.

Blue lights arrived. Twice, a police woman with white, opaque, Lucite Elvis Costello glasses asked me questions.

One day, my drug dealer, Mikey—he sat on my kitchen counter and stole $140 from my wallet, money beyond my deal.

All three convenience stores around here seem to have a "zero nutrition" policy. Men with nothing spend sixteen dollars on scratch-off lottery cards, thinking they're going to walk out rich.

I am white and Spike Lee has labeled me "a devil." I've heard the word "gentrification" somehow, here and there.

There's an unkempt house with a Confederate flag and on that, a circle with writing in it. I cross the street when passing it on my way to the post office, thinking an old drunk is alone in there, sitting at the kitchen table, cleaning his beloved Colt.

There are no bugs in my house.

And the roof doesn't leak.

I've been finishing up my next two books and I'm pretty much spent, but I'll be on-stage in New Orleans at the Maple Leaf Bar on Oak Street in thirty-six hours.

— Pensacola, October 17, 2018

A Closer Look

Seth
I've got it!
You're a folk hero, man…
The whole thing is so dangerously dysfunctional and
    wholly stupid
And you are there and on it
Nightly
When you and the wife take a few weeks
Away from studio and stage
I come to resent it
I need my Seth…

And who cares if you're really a paleolithic "radar" character
    named "Vaugg?"

Dig?

I'm a writer and a singer and a member of the Justice League
Also known as the League of Justice
Sometimes I promise myself I'll write down some of your
    opening monologue
Because it's extraordinarily revealing and concise
Many a time during "A Closer Look"
I've sat there thinking
That's brave, man!

And that bravery doesn't necessarily register with the people
And the other half call it "fake news"
You've kept us on the tracks and off the rocks, Seth
And I, for one, am grateful

Seth Meyers
Y' done good for us through these years
And for unexpected events…
And Groundhog Day…
Please bring back the captain and duckie and the mermaid

That's Seth…
The guy reading on the sofa over there

Vaugg rules!

And … Fred Armisen has gotten the most attention any amateur musician has ever gathered … other than me

And this has been a closer look…

BATH DRAIN

The bath drain on top
Doesn't hardly do
If you set a bath and walk into the other room
And the phone rings
And you carry on a 25-minute conversation with your editor in Pensacola
A slight tapping puddle at your casual step reminds you…
Oh, no no no! Not again!

This has happened to me four times this year
The bedding is stripped
And immediately dispatched to the bathroom area
You may or may not have changed the bedding sometime in the last few days …or weeks
Uh…
All towels and socks and extras are thrown in the mush
Cassette tapes and writing folders, too

Deep breath…
Okay…
That little drain
Doesn't hardly do

My Hollywood Ladies

She ain't you but she's here and she's got that dark rhythm in her soul[1]
Penelope Cruz
Walk 1200 miles of trail through Patagonia
And that's what you'll find
Patty Smith...
In New York subway
Rail-thin in peacoat
Composition book under arm
Danica Patrick losing the helmet
Angelica Houston
Black coffee in bed
Frances McDormand has a soft side at dawn
Joan Baez at the mic
Alone in the spotlight
As sad as the song
Bo Derek in the river
Speaking to silent Tarzan
Janice Joplin topless in beads
Jennifer Gray
The pout before the smile
Catherine Keener...
All scatter!
Cheryl Crow in Daisy Dukes and cowboy boots comin' after me

1 Bob Dylan, "Brownesville Girl," *Knocked-Out Loaded*. Columbia Records, 1986

Dustbowl woman with clinging children
Ladybird Johnson
The face and the name … and the bonnet, dear
Minnie Driver
Ritorna da me, mi amor!
Ritorna da me!
Karen Silkwood's black leather jacket
Nathalie Portman…
Fly on my sweet angel
Fly on through the sky[2]
Tori Amos plays in the lobby of the Sussex Inn (to dust it off)
Frances Conroy
If God is a woman…?
Sheila E in the parlor with a drumstick at midnight
BAMM Shaka-laka-laka BAMM!
Linda McCartney
Irreplaceable
Giselle Fernandez
Where are you?
Robin Wright
Has *the cutest* nostrils
So do Jessica Lange and Madonna
Glenn Close
Oh!
Elaine Welteroth
I see you, Elaine!

---

[2] The Jimi Hendrix Experience, "Fly on My Sweet Angel," *The Cry of Love*, Reprise records, 1971

Lieutenant Jeffries
She's the real, true motherly figure in Dali's "Child Watching Birth of New Man"
Now you know
Iman
Wouldn't let her husband smoke in the house
Amy Klobuchar
I keep thinkin' of her in faded denim…
And a choker
E.D. Falco
Never turn your back on a woman with two or more initials in her first name
Patricia Neal
HUD's Phantom
Her wide-set eyes
Pregnant Demi Moore
Stretch marks are best smoothed by gentle nibbles…
But you know that, Demi
Isabella Rosalini
What is it about her that makes you crave a plate of soft-shell crabs?
Linda Lavin
Alice, please tell Mel that he can kiss my grits!
For Amy Winehouse, a candle … and all my love
Chrissie Hynde
"Hymn to Her"
Ellen Barkin
See the sun shine!
Maya Rudolph in *Tortilla Soup* …

16 — Maiche Lev

That's her?
Alicia Keys
Mountain child
It's her island and the great ocean is listening
Valeria Golino
Solo la verdad
Hilary Swank
Plain she is not

My Other Latest Smallest (Old Remote Controls)

To crisscross the nation
Locating hundreds of junk shops
Collecting old TV remotes
Goodwill always has a big, useless box of 'em
A few hundred could be obtained easily
A brush with some all-purpose cleanser
Could get the éclair-shaped devices back to their original,
   black, glossy splendor
Then to simply glue them end-to-end
On a 4x4-foot square of plywood
Painted black
And you've got a one-of-a-kind visual for any living room
First apartment or swanky bachelor pad
An attention-winning conversation piece
Mosaics in Sony, RCA, Samsung … or *whatever!*

"You guys always find the coolest stuff"

Poor Girl

Oh Mia…
You've suffered

All those others in their automobiles
Headed for lit rooms with feather quilts
They never have and never will suffer your predicament
Homelessness
Ten years gone
Ten years spent

Mia
They dealt with education
Your seven years in Gainesville
With eyes wide-shut

In a *putrid* tee-shirt
At that Italian place you said your ma used to take you to
You said you consider the working world to be "retarded"
Dirty socks under flip-flops
What brand of sorrow is this?
The homeless
The departed

And Mia…
Those people out there in their cars

They think to themselves
Poor girl
Poor, poor girl
What if I landed in a place like that?

My house
Secure
Clean and locked
Warm and stocked
My children coming into their own
He's her husband
She's his wife
Girl Scouts
Skateboards
Summer camp
College
Secure
Clean and locked

Look at that poor girl
She's fallen through the cracks of the world
Dirty, disheveled, and mean
Could be anyone
Could be me
Prostitution
I always see her on these streets
These corners

These sidewalks
Her eyes are angry
That little radio she keeps to her ear
She must sleep on the beach
Or on the leaves under the trees in the park

How do you land there?
Everybody's got a story…
But *how?*

Has nothing she calls her own
She wakes outside day after day
She's pretty
She's a beauty
She's without a home
Mia
You've suffered…
And before you practiced personal defamation and
     character assassination…

Mia…
I liked it so when you'd speak…
When you'd just speak
How you've suffered

STRUMMER

All the best punk rockers had cracked teeth

I don't trust you…
Why do you trust me?
Daddy was a bank robber
But he never hurt nobody
He just loved to live that way
And he loved to steal your money

I always felt like I was inferior
And then I heard the Sex Pistols
What a great group!
Suddenly I knew…
It didn't have to matter that much

You know what they said…
Well, some of it was true

And everybody's sittin' 'round watchin' television!

I got my motorcycle jacket but I'm walking all the time

Siiiiiiid

ZION

Boy…
What was it you said to me last time I's there
    a few years back?
"Gotta dream while y' can?"

So, it's been a awhile
Have you developed a club act?
Miami?
New York?
Los Angeles…?
The man!

In Gainesville you'd have finished your fourth year by
    now, right?
And you'd be headed for junior professorship and serious
    graduate work somewhere

But you're back
Waking up in the room next to your daddy
With all your credits freshly buried

A Dade boy soon at least has a place all his own

Zion…
Get back on the train
It goes everywhere, kid

THESE POOR PEOPLE

These poor people are never gonna drive
A brand-spankin'-new, royal blue Chevrolet Corvette
And these poor people are never gonna
Take a gauche, oceanic, five-star summer trip

These folks are never gonna have designer jeans in
    their closet
They're never gonna get it together
And go back to junior college

This meager lot will never speak a sentence of the Queen's
    English, eloquent
Nor will they pay notice to their declining health
Change their abysmal diet

They don't bicycle across the country
They don't fish for marlin offshore
They don't own a business of any sort
Other than maybe some lawn mowers
Grassed and greasy
Trailer worn
Truck beat t' shit

These ghetto dwellers never set eyes on the Grand Canyon in
    the west
They don't go to summer camp in North Carolina

They rarely sit down as a family at a table nicely set
Except for blessed family reunions
They never get out of East Hackensack

Here they are at the Happy Shopper convenience store
Spending money on Lotto that they don't have to spend
There is nothing nutritious in this whole place…
Nothing
Old men congregate outside
Scratching at the cards

I won $400 once
I mean … you can win!

The con never ends
The con…
No…
It never ends

I Was in Bed

I was in bed when Katrina passed over
I woke up
My head on some linen
Or a sleeping bag by the jalousie windows
Six feet from parked cars in the cul de sac by Biscayne Bay
Suddenly a mature banyan tree filled up with wind
Like it had taken a deep breath...

I awoke

It was nighttime
Rattling, flickering fluorescents...
Oh, is this the hurricane?

That tree went down
And what a sad, sorry thing it is
To see that mighty disc of root and dirt upended
But I'll tell you...
A great banyan reminds you of what weather really is

On Top of Africa Hot

Two hundred and fifty-some elephants die off at once in a
   Central African preserve
What was the temperature reading?
A hideous death for grand pachyderms
And 250 all in a row looks like…
Nothing else … ever

Maladjustment

Sometimes people don't adjust well
Somehow ... somewhere
Somebody must've kicked 'em around some[3]
Too harsh a punishment
Too hard a lesson
World in motion
Some fall through the cracks
Coming to ... no position

If y' steal the innocence from a kid
What have you taken?
What's over before it had a chance to begin?

Some people's paths in this world are sheltered
Some meet up with the wicked
Some parents fought drunk
Some didn't
What comes of it?
The heart?
The spirit?
Over and over again
Slamming doors

And...

---

3 Tom Petty and the Heartbreakers, "Refugee," *Damn the Torpedoes*, MCA Records, 1979

The abused come to abuse
That's how it is
Learned behaviours
Coping mechanisms
We emulate
Broken promises
Little secrets
Sad truths
A house of love
A house of pain
Dilapidated floors
Tattered roofs

Maladjusted
Acting out at school
Latchkey kids
Idle time
Puberty
Nature
Unsupervised
Pornography's influence…
What transpires?
It happens as easy as…
A toolbox holds tools
Everyone looking down saying, "Now what?
Nothing is the same as it was

Maladjustment...
Seventeen Magazine
Self-image
Many feel they're not worthy of love
If only I could be friends with Jennifer
It's a rough road any way you spin it
Standards

You're not smooth enough
Got a weak chin
Jenn is *somethin'*
Leanin' there on her boyfriend
I'll set my sights on changing this nose
I'll change my hair so many times...
I'll ... *fit in*
Well, the doctor says
"If there's something you don't like about your face..."
Ma...
Am I alright?

Maladjustment
Some people don't adjust well
Juicy juice
Doodle chips
365 days a year
Coca-Cola is great...
Except there's sixteen teaspoons of sugar in every can

That's a lot of fucking sugar
Does this make me a bad American?
Somebody gimme a cheeseburger!

Some people don't adjust well…
Some folks are always in a bad way
Leave me alone
Leave me alone in my misery
Go away!
Nothin' that hurts gonna last forever…
Unless you let it
Another busy day
Come what may
Come what may

FACTOID

There are secretions in the human body that can melt a nail

WE CAN'T DO IT

"We can't do it"
That's what Trump said in response to the minimum wage
   being raised to $15 an hour

In proportion to the growth in our economy since the
   early seventies
Minimum wage should be over twenty dollars

ST. VINCENT BEACH

He decided to live on his bike for a while
Boxed up everything worth its space in storage
Primped the apartment for departure
Took a lesson from the Fuji bicycle sales floor
On how to change a tire
And…
With four saddlebags and a two-wheeled trailer behind
He went!
A pop-up tent
A few blankets
His wet-suit (that still fits)
And a stack of lyrics, laminated
None written prior to 1974
And he pedaled off with those dastardly, confining
    cramp-ons for pedals

On the road
Between his editor and the Apalachicola lifeguard stands
With a solar battery pack
He completed his last two books in the sand

He stayed out a while
Sometimes working labor pools up and down the state
He managed to save a buck
And he retrieved his boxes from storage

And he flew away to St. Vincent Beach
The Philippines
In search of that unattractive woman
Who might truly stir his soul

Fabio

Why wouldn't I do TV?
Well, there might be women out there
Who think I'm Matthew McConaughey, y' know?
I've got a face for radio, man

Buddy Hacket doesn't scare me
And half a scruffed-up Dustin Hoffman might break the ice

LUCILLE

Lucille!
First I have to tell you
I had your handwriting analyzed
By a *strange* gypsy woman
She says that although you seem to be
A mild-mannered American grad student
In fact, you are fit to wear mink
White against those dark eyes
Your thumbs upping the collar
Diamonds hanging down
An ice palace your own

Lucille!
You're too fine for me, baby
Much too fine…
Lucille!

LOVE

Love your suit … and those shoes
And I love your glasses
Great choice!
I love it when you call me names
I love a woman with a little monkey in her
You can't hurry love…
I wanna know what love is
Love, Love, Love
Love is a many-splendored thing
Love is like oxygen…
Love hurts…
Love is more than just a feelgood emotion
Who luvs mummi?
He loves his bike
He's on it somewhere out in the US right now
I guess that's the price of love
I know it's not cheap
Love the one you're with
I love you; you love me…
I love you…
I honestly love you
Love God first
For the love of God, man!
If you love somebody, set them free
I love Lucy

Love me tender…
You give love a bad name
Love my way…
It' a new road
Love makes the world go 'round
Aren't we still in love
When you're in love with a beautiful woman…
Y' can't make love all by yourself
Maybe someday when you're by yourself alone
You'll know the love I had for you was never my own
Losing love is like a window in your heart…
Love … soft as an easy chair
Love and mercy
That's what we need tonight
Gay love
Subaru love
Fairytale love affair
Poison love
Muskrat love
A "love-in"
Love can mend your life but love can break your heart
Love American Style
Lovers
It's only love and that is all…
Ain't talkin 'bout love!
This kind of love … I'm so sick of it
Love Story

Courtney Love

Love grows where my Rosemary goes

Dr. Lovejoy

What's love got to do with it?

Nothing says love like stalking

America—Love it or leave it

A mother's love

My love belongs to my wife

DYLAN LIVE

What do I like about Bob Dylan most?
His contained aggression
His authority
His humanity
His tear
His non-encroaching demeanor
His encroaching demeanor
His style
His warning
His forbearance
His occasional smile
His insane laugh
His turquoise blue eyes
His curly mop
His well-planted profanity
His impatience
His contempt for fools
His seethe at evil
His whipping pace
His worn heart
His actual dread
His Christian love
He's not as kind and forgiving as he seems
His courage
His concert in Huntsville last week
His tempest

52 — Maiche Lev

His harem
His minion

What do I like most about Bob Dylan?
What goes into his voice

I don't care how big you think you are…
History is just gonna roll right over you
And yes, the most reviled disciple has no saint
Sean Penn narrates his book *Chronicles* so well
Bootleg Series III, disc III
If *Revelations* had a soundtrack it'd probably sound like some
    of that, Buster

SOMEONE ELSE

Someone else knows you better than you know yourself
Someone else can tell better what you'll do next
Someone else knows your strengths and weaknesses
Someone else is mindful of your greater benevolence
Someone else offers higher assistance

Someone else knows where you've been
Who you are and what games you've played in
Someone else whispers in the wings
Someone else…
Here you were a thief
Here an angel weeping

Someone else tells you who's a backstabber
Someone else in your heart and mind
Someone else wants you to know what really matters
Someone else follows you on the path
And is with you as you read the signs

Someone else prays you take pity on yourself
Someone else perceives your dissonance
The milk of human kindness
Someone else was assigned to you
In a holy faithfulness

54 — Maiche Lev

Someone else sees through your walls
And knows you're hurting
Someone else knows what's bright ahead
If only what you were clinging to
Was what you were deserting

Someone else asks if you can see yourself
As clearly as someone who's had you on his mind, friend
If my hands are tied
Must I not wonder within
Who tied them and why
And where must I have been?[4]

Someone else

---

4 Bob Dylan, "What Good Am I?" *Oh Mercy,* Columbia Records, 1989

Genealogy

We like to believe otherwise
But your genealogy is as wet as the day it was poured

NERDY

The act of entering and achieving in a classroom
Leads to a lifelong love of learning

The act of entering *into* and achieving *in* a classroom
Leads to a lifelong love of learning

DUNGEONS AND DRAGONS

A game that makes a kid stand up and declare, "Victory!"
Fists to the table
Head held high

DEAR ME

Oh, dear me…
You say through it all I turned out to be a man
Well…
If you gotta go through what I been through to earn
    that label…
You can put me in a rocket ship
With a few chimpanzees
Make sure there's enough fuel
For us to find a motel somewhere
And make sure there's plenty of tuna fish on board

And don't forget the can opener!

IF YOU KNEW

If you knew you had issues that were recurring
And that you needed help with them
And you sought out a psychiatrist
To uncover and explore your hang-ups

And then after about a year of counseling
The doctor handed you a bio
Just about so thick
Telling you that you no longer needed to be a patient

And you read it
And it made you think
And feel generally pleased
But for a few uncomfortable necessaries…

Well then…
That would be money well-spent
Don't you agree?

Then…
You wouldn't have to walk across America all by yourself
Alone
Nor would you have to dream
About owning too big or too fast a boat

64 — Maiche Lev

The perfect woman in your past
Who took up with your best friend
Was not a viable reason for leaving town

Your obsession with her
Has led you into dire straits
Take up with someone
A man must be a man, Maiche

You would also accept that it's okay…
You don't have to be Bruce Springsteen
And the pornography addiction was shallow and
    damaging after all

And the moment you exposed your pee-pee
To Laurie Goodiss in the seventh grade
Shouldn't still make you squirm

Your enthusiastic attraction to Black women
Could be something to pursue
Why not…?

The fact that you're balding
Shouldn't cause such emotional tumult
It's a detriment to suffer it

The LSD insanity
Twenty-five years ago

Was something positively left behind

Your need for constant distraction
Can be alleviated by better physical maintenance

Children move on
They don't want to hear the sense you have to make that
    much any more

Men, too, can light a lot of candles
It invites solemnity

And Maiche…
The cassette with those songs you gave me
Was surprisingly good
Keep enjoying your voice
As you're wont to

And lose those seventeen pounds
That keep you in a state of poor self-image

Your idea of going to cooking school…
Great idea!
(and big pussy magnet, Maiche!)

Your hostility toward hypermasculinity is understandable in
    this day and age
But that anger can waste a lot of energy

And in how many sessions did we speak of
   "psychosomatic illness?"
It's so simple…
And yet few can conceive

It has been a pleasure and a wonder
To be your doctor, Maiche

Always,

Dr. Eli Levy '84–'85
Dr. Frank Bolea '87
Dr. Juan B. Espinoza '89–'99
Dr. Rascha Lawrence '16–'19

—Maiche

LETTER TO A LONG-TERM JUNKIE

JP...
I know you've heard it all
And there's very little anyone can tell you
It's just that there's something precious about you
That your dangerous way of living does not respect
Strong medicine for deep pain, Jen

You were *someone* to me...
Your big blue eyes
Your graham cracker skin
Your powers of observation and response
Your laughter
Your divine frame

The endless drama
The constant lying
You've seen it all
You've known it all
You've done it all
What gave you license?
We never knew what was gonna happen next

And now you're gone
Left us this heartache
Jennifer Prusiensky (1979–2020)
She was more than she was

BE GOOD TO SOMEONE

Be good to someone
Maybe you'll get a little love out o' this life
If you're cold and you curse…
Once you wanted to be husband and wife

Be good to someone
You can always make things worse
Don't keep a knife in your pocket
Don't put a hammer in your purse

Be good to someone
Even when they're nasty to you
They say, "Go check into a hotel!"
A little space will do
Don't be cruel
Call your fighting days through

Be good to someone
It might be tough for a while
Accept some guilt
Suspend the trial

Be good to someone
Even if they can't be good to you
When all's in a rut

70 — Maiche Lev

Don't give up
Yes, serve one another
To make it right again
To make it good

I feel like spaghetti…
Pasta pomodoro

What You Never Forget

You never forget how to fold a paper airplane
You never your first lemonade stand
You never forget looking out on Wrigley Field
You never forget standing before a deep blue ocean
You never forget getting your driver's license
You never forget your first kiss
You never forget finding out what your place in the world is
You never forget getting caught in a lie
And how you went to cover it up like a child would try
You never wash away some regrets
Some things will always take your breath away
You never forget your mother's love
Search for it you will until your dying day
You never forget how others saw where things were going
And then there it went
You never forget taking a fall
You never forget the cheap way big money is spent
You never forget how you end up floored at not letting
    things lie
You never forget certain dreams
Some you can live with; some you can't
Y' never forget being broke
Y' never forget catching your first fish
How it felt tugging the rod
And how y' had to muscle it in
I guess y' never forget the first time you're arrested

The cuffs are too tight
The lack of air in the car
You wish it was over
You're thrown in with the others

So, what would anyone say they could never forget?
John F. Kennedy's assassination — November 22, 1963
Dr. Martin Luther King Junior's "I have a Dream" Speech at
   the Lincoln Memorial — August 28, 1963

Y' never forget the '83 Camaro's smooth, streamlined look
Or how the '80 Firebird's front end didn't and never
   would work
Y' never forget Micheal Jordan's flight from the
   free-throw line
Y' never forget Dan Marino's guns
Y' never forget Dale Earnhardt's rally
Or Pelé's rainbow
Or Phelps's gold
Jack Nicklaus
The golden bear
Lee Trevino in black
Payne Stewart's argyles
Ahhh … Seve Ballesteros … *Arrêt*
Sandy Kofax
Catfish Hunter
Joe DiMaggio
Phyllis Diller!

Meyer Boy (My Sister's Dog)

Hrrmmff…
You Schleins…
You were easy to believe in
Yes, you were just that
And I don't know when I'm going to doggie heaven
But I know that God has made a little room for me there
And I wouldn't mind at all serving you again
Being in your rooms and at your knee
You gave me shelter and care
And attention and love
What creature on earth could ask for more?

I'll check on Misty when I get there
That darned cat!
And I'll send you a dream
A sweet dream from the heart

And I don't know if I should tell you…
But I never did like the name 'Meyer' much
But it's ok…
You were easy to believe in
You blessed me

— Meyer

CHUCK MANGIONE (PRE-DIGITAL)

Wanna know what's amazing?
Finding Chuck Mangione records
Like all great music
His was *honed*
His bandmates surrounded him
All as good as any heavy session guys
Mangione
It's so worth it to your ears
There's not a single glossy, overproduced song in there

1976
It was the end of a way of recording sound
The drums were mic'd
Everything had depth
The guitars were so clean!
So thanks, Chuck!
And thanks to the boys!
I've got five or six new movements to fill my place with

Smile

What's in that smile?

California Sunkist
Uruguayan *maís*
A string of Russian horses in the snow
Africa wide
Time itself
Two rows side by side
Arabian sand
Arabian nights
The Arabian moon
Oh, the stars
Twinkling gems
Oh, Jerusalem

Marvin Gaye

Y' know what Marvin Gaye's face says?
Marvin Gaye's face says that the heavens are turning on more
   than one axis

Someday, Then and There

Almost looks like the continent of Africa
Is a desalinization plant waiting to be activated
Seems to me the land mass Australia
Needs something to drink
She's dehydrated
Sweden
Norway
Spain and France
Are one long soap dish on the basin
The sink
The Mediterranean's a urinal puck
Half-disintegrated
Blue, white, or pink?

Russia…
Well, could be hell did freeze over
So many time zones
It's the world's whole other half
Someone said, "It ain't climate change
It's climate collapse!"

Old England is an abscess in need of a lance
Ireland?
One dirty old town
It don't know why it do
But it dance

Iceland is home to only elves and gnomes
You end up there when y' fall through a trapdoor
In one of Bill Gates' awesome homes

Moving right along now…

Greenland was purchased by Jimmy Buffett
For a dozen glazed donuts
A large coffee with two creams
The Amazon River's over here somewhere if I'm
    not mistaken…
Right up here near the Philippines

Who's ever heard of British Columbia?
I'll chop down every tree in Canada
Burn 'em up in a pile for fun

America…
Has that certain somethin'
Every time she smiles
(I pledge allegiance…)

Honduras and Belize
Guatemala and Mexico
Like an umbilical cord
For Curly, Larry, and Moe

Panama
Ecuador
Brazil
Argentina
Lots of trees and undiscovered species
Pass the *cholula* please

Way down below...
It's hard to spell 'Antarctica'
This popsicle I hold
Is from the last chunk of ice
Taken from the last glacier
Receding from the slopes of Patagonia
Mmmmm ... grape!

Hawaii
Waikiki
Honolulu
Ashtabula
What time is it?
Excuse me; do you have the ti*me, sir?*

My first name is Apothecary
My last name is Bromeliad
Let them eat cake made of centipedes
High in protein
Anyone complains, send 'em to me

In Japan
In Kobe Town…
I'll open up an Outback
Spread my wealth around
A place where the McRib is always back!

There are nearly ten-billion human beings
Walking upright upon this Earth
Every last one of 'em came from a woman giving birth
Every one of 'em…
Upright
That's right
There's only one creature that does so step
You only live once?
Well…
That would be a pretty shallow and desperate ponderance
Upright
Homo erectus
Reténte ebullience

CROWD ROARS

Bell rung

Crowd roars

Clotheslined

Crowd roars

Body slam

Crowd roars

Into the wall

Crowd roars

Chewie, the hyperdrive!

Crowd roars

"We won't get fooled again!" … *No no!*

Crowd roars

Bitch slapped

Crowd roars

Drilled ass

Crowd roars

The Exorcist

Crowd roars

Boss time

It's all coming back to me now

SMOKING CRACK WITH DENNIS MILLER ON A SUNDAY MORNING

You haven't arrived
Until you've taken a hammer to the head from Dennis Miller
It's worse than a little bad press
Dennis 'll bust you up and break you down
In three staggered sentences
And he's *right*
Faceless fucking assassin misanthrope comic genius
    that he is

It was almost ten years ago
Through the static of a little clock-radio in Jacksonville
I found him on a show broadcast out of ... Halifax?
And this morning
A decade later
There he is on the TV
Just as informed
Just as great
Just as purposefully controversial

I know he's got George Carlin tattooed somewhere on
    his body
And *no one* worked as hard as George Carlin
To keep the weapon clean and greased

Dennis Miller
He's got somethin' for ya
Like just this Sunday morning he said
"Trump ... I heard a report that he was born in Kenya!"
Dennis Miller
Motherfucker all the way

SURPRISES

Someone's got a surprise for me
Who could it be?
What could it be?
Is it another writing pad to work on?
They make pretty good frisbees if you throw them from the
    hip ... sidearm
This surprise...
Is it an important business proposition?
Is it an invitation to a royal coronation of a daughter of one
    of the sons of Zion?

Surprise!
Someone has taken my poems and set them to music!
Available on vinyl
Cassette
Compact disc

A surprise for me...
Heard it from a little birdie last Tuesday or Wednesday
Have I become the inheritor of a grand, sprawling house?
Or a quaint little cottage on the beach?
Maybe a big, glassy New York City apartment?
Are the walls covered with art someone's collected?
Do I have a book deal with Simon and Schuster or Knopff?
Or some skinny independent?

A surprise!
A secret
It was all a bad dream, Maiche
Your love interest hasn't sold her ass to the president
Your application for overseas citizenship has been accepted
Your prayers have been answered and implemented
All the lessons so hard to bear have been with merciful understanding documented
The wicked witch and the one from the west have been reconciled
And are now practically related
I'm not spoiling the surprise, am I?
That little bird must 've known I was in need of some good news
Something to be almost celebrated…

Oh, look!
A piñata!
And all my friends!
A blindfold
And a donkey's butt
And a birthday cake
My favorite flavor—pralines and cream
Pralines and cream!
I'm so excited
Ribbons and balloons
Giftwrap and paper plates and plastic forks and plastic spoons

Surprise!
We love you, Maiche...!

A pony!
An electric car!
A big, yellow guitar!
A tennis racquet!
A huge jar of jelly beans
A new set of drums
A large-screen TV
All for me!
And a ... and a ... puppy!?

All of my friends
You can go home now
Really...
Bye!

Just a Song Before I Go

Just a song before I go
To whom it may concern
Travelling twice the speed of sound
It's easy to get burned[5]

---

5   Crosby, Stills, and Nash. "Just a Song Before I Go," *CSN*, Atlantic Records, 1977

THE LIFE WITHIN

Y' know
When you've suffered a long illness
And you're better
And the discomfort has passed
You're so thankful for your life and your health
It's weightless
Perfect light

The same is true when a friend or a loved one dies
Suddenly you know and feel
That a human being is so blessed a creature
We live so free
So long
Godly

Yet we expire
Like any organism out there
Our lifetimes
Death seems like a dirty trick
Resolutions in hospital rooms

The life within us
A holy thing

LOVING AND LAUGHTER

Love is gained in confidence
Trust in another's decency and conscience
A few laughs on a slow afternoon
Goes a long way

ON FATHER'S DAY (WITH D. BRICKER)

On this Father's Day
An image my father's father must have encountered
His son
Someone his own
Streamlined
Beautified to the world
His culture
His family

Seventeen with wheels…
Something so wild could have escaped from the zoo!
Smoking
Gambling
Strutting
And whoring with a smile
Slick!

My grandfather
His son
My father

Call your daddy on Father's Day
Or send him a note
All of you is a semblance of him

And what the aged crave is union

It's good to hear your voice, Dad

And son, you sound like you're doin' something right for yourself

Dad...
I wanted to tell you that I remember some of the stuff we did...
And that we did a lot in the garage and out back by the canal
And I remember...
So happy Father's Day, old man

Good Sex

If the genitals were for healing
What would good sex be?

You're into Me Like...

Baby, you're into me

Like a bag of groceries left in the car

Maybe overnight…

What to keep?

What to throw away?

Or maybe they been sittin' just an hour

The milk…

What do you think?

Or maybe the tilapia under the passenger seat starts to get
  ripe on Wednesday

Oh my God!

I knew it had to be something!

HA EISHA SABRA

I've thought of you more than you've thought of me
Don't start, Maiche
In my life and times, I've loved you more
Oh, my Romeo, tell me…
I've gone home alone for twenty years
Slept alone in my bed
That's noble … and sad
I've been loyal for the sake of loyalty
What does that mean?
It means you've meant everything to me, lady
Well that deserves a kiss, my Maichy doggy daddy

Sweetness…
Talk to me in your mother tongue
Thoughtlessly
Foolishly
Circle me speaking musically
Be here with me
Yes…
Be here with me

STALKING IS...

To stalk
To spy
To lie in wait
To follow
Something of menacing overtone
Silently observing
To frighten
To harass
To terrorize
To stalk

Your Honor
I flouted the law
Officers asked me not to come to the big store — the CVS
But I did

We spoke
With Miss Ryazantseva present
It was in the afternoon
The officer told me I'd become a nuisance
By continually putting cute items on Alina's car...
A few baby mangoes in mango season
Folded up letters
Dialogue for a kid's book I'd been inspired to write
And bread from the supermarket in its bag
Bread?

She's Russian
I thought maybe that's what people in her mother country
    did to say, "Hi"

To stalk
In almost all of these casual deliveries
I left two pennies
All I ever requested was a lunch date
To ask twenty questions and put my two cents in
I went into her place of employment only a few times over the
    months…
Like twice
In the comings and goings
We never even had half a conversation

To stalk
So again, your Honor
After being told by the officer not to return for a year
And to keep my distance
I asked the officer if I could send a drone over
He smiled
Smoke signals?
How about a singing telegram, officer?
Oh, skywriting! Of course!
We both busted out laughing
Alina didn't know what to think
She asked me if I was homeless

To stalk
That week my new book arrived
I thought I'd deliver one to Alina
In a specially-decorated envelope
With beads and glitter and markers and cute little things…
I delivered it to a side counter
Dropped it where it would be found
And left
A day or two later I returned
Thinking maybe I'd been legitimized
Maybe she'd have lunch with someone who could write a book of some sort

Stalking
I was wrong and I am sorry for having upset anyone
Please accept my apology
As I offer it to Miss Ryazantseva
An unmarried woman

In my mind
I am not today nor have I ever been a stalker
Though if I was riding by on my bicycle
I'd say, "Hi!"
This happened once
I was returning to my cottage from the train about ten o'clock
I saw her at her car and I rode over
I frightened her…

And I apologized
I am no stalker
Just another lonely guy

To stalk
Three days in jail
Three days in the psych ward
For what?
I am no stalker
But I understood
On my second day in jail
Staring at a dry, spit-strewn wall
I realized I'd scared someone
And it's the job of the State to protect her
A loaf of pumpernickel stuffed in your sideview mirror
 doesn't happen every day…
And I'm sorry for that
I really am…
I scared someone
My apologies
My two cents in

Find Your Way Back

I'm not on a life raft in the middle of the ocean
I'm not on a starship that flosses your teeth
I'm not watching the first star that rises over the desert
I'm not climbing a boulder sittin' on a mountainside
I'm not what's hidden underneath
I'm not mowing a manicured yard in Connecticut
I'm not in a jungle where everything crawls
I'm not in an old-growth forest, clear-cut for miles
I'm not in a Texas-sized plastic dump in the Pacific, afloat
I'm not stuck in all that permafrost up north
Or watching what happens as it thaws
I'm not in that cotton field
Or in that rolling vineyard
I'm not lost with the witch of the forest
I'm not out in those Big Island swells
I'm not plush at home
In front of my sixty-one-inch Samsung

No…
I'm here off Quito 'neath a palm in the sun
With a whole half a toothache that just won't quit

BEWARE

Beware of people with nothing to lose
They'll put God up against the wall
Offer their heads for a prayer
They've been schooled by fools
Iced by icons
Armed by amateurs
One's sittin' next to you there

Those with nothing to lose
They pray at will for keeps
It's all the way
All the time…
They're standing there grinning
Always on the side that's winning

Beware

WHISTLING A TUNE
(WITH DAVE BRICKER)

What's the sound of the song I sing that I never get out?
This tune…
I can feel it
I can hear it
Above a murmur
Almost an anthem
See the choir sway
Hear the choir shout
A sweet melody
It's on the tip of my tongue
Scared to my soul it'll leave my memory

It's a plea for mercy
A declaration of love
Power
Weakness
I'm whistlin' a tune
In my Argyles
Somewhere above

Cakewalking with Claude Debussy
More cowbell with Herb Alpert
Rave on with Buddy Holly
Elton John comes on
It's okay to say your feelings are hurt

A piano by a window overlooking the city long after dark
A kid kicking a can down the street
A big Magnavox
A magical box full of parts

A catchy phrase
Radio days
Chipmunks
Daylight come and me wan' go home
There's a hole in the bucket
Jingles
Ditties
Limbo lot

The tune I know but can't get out...
It comes
It does
In some way it's devout
I'll prove it to you
Everybody's building the big ships and the boats
Some are building monuments
Others jotting down notes[6]

Come on without...
Come on within

---

6 Bob Dylan, "Mighty Quinn," *Self Portrait,* Columbia Records, 1970

GENDER REASSIGNMENT

What kind of crippling need is met by sex
   reassignment surgery?

I am not an authority on the subject
My opinions and perspectives are not vast and varied
But they're topical
I'm a layman
I have only the simplest interpretation
It's in the news these days
LGBTQ

The human intellect is a huge phenomenon
Lots of room to carry lots of weight around
And one thing's for sure about the human subject:
It never knew what it was going to hand itself next

People get an idea in their head
An answer
A cure…
They carry it with 'em from when they rise
Till evening offers its rest

I believe the man who says he's always felt like a woman
   trapped in a man's body
And likewise the female who's never identified comfortably
   with her femininity

The latter is more than just given to the effeminate
The former
In boots and jeans
Her natural affects
She's a *he* in so much that she's...
Forgive me...
Broad and butch
And he's a *she*...
Takes after his mama
In feature and in touch

So sex reassignment...
It makes sense; you're worth it
It's an answer to the obsession
A completion...
What it all means
Both have awakened in many seasons
With these all-consuming dreams

I was listening to a talk show on the radio
A doctor said...
It doesn't work...
It doesn't make you into the other sex
You're still that much a woman or a man
Who you've always been
The suicide rate in the trans-gender community
Is 20% higher than the rest of the population

And I learned further that the sex change, once complete
Renders the person far less able to achieve orgasm
And that the physical alteration leads to panic at first
It's nothing!
It's nothing!
A very real depression sets in

These are indeed serious issues
Worse than a case of the blues
You thought you were opening up a candy store
But suddenly you're not so enamored of being crowned "royalty" at the rave
Cradle to grave
Cradle to grave
Same shit; different day
Only you can't get off
And you can't unring the bell

Things aren't so funny
Who's anyone to call anyone else "a deviant" or "sick?"
What is…
Or what makes someone a "misfit?"

Having completed the surgery
You leave the hospital *different*
The build-up
The let-down

What was it?
This was it
Permanent disfigurement

I hope this doesn't come off as mocking or cruel
She never would wear pink
His role model early-on was his big sister
His favorite place to hide
Was his mother's closet
Brushes and makeup around the bathroom sink

Everyone has a dance in their lives
A mad little step that's all their own
And isn't it ironic?
A man who changes into a woman finds out
A woman's life is often a less-than-glamorous event
And she who chooses to become a man finds out
That power and lust are less than a transcendental
   occurrence

A sex change operation
Is about the heaviest thing you can allow to happen
   to yourself
You tell yourself something long enough…
You're just bound to believe it's true

The doctors who take your wad of money are so congenial
The order of your existence itself is breached

They take you out the front door in a wheelchair — standard
The emotional consequences are unforgiving and lasting
More serious than you bargained for
You were expecting a whole new beginning
Your corporeality is as familiar to you as the eyes sitting in your head...
The blood in your veins...
The voice you hear yourself speak with...

Your years of pissy attitude culminate in a cruel, irresponsible trick
Some will read this and weep
Some will curse me

What kind of crippling need is met by gender reassignment surgery?
It doesn't work
I am not an authority on the subject
But eventually someone in your life takes the step

You think of something for a long, long time...
The seriousness of surgical metamorphosis is inextricably more serious than the waiver the good doctor has you sign
There's only so much that the human mind can endure...

Across the hall two queens bitch as they dress to go
You take this drastic measure
What isn't a joke any more...

You hear on the news how trans people are being victimized
People with bad attitudes aggrandize themselves by
   committing murder
Are they threatened?
What drives them?
What phobia?
What superstition?

Becoming transsexual
Is a step into the unknown

A Voter

You know now how you knew then
Four more years wasn't gonna happen

You know now how you knew then
Four more years wasn't gonna happen
'Cause you went out and voted

FOR DARREN

Darren Linksman and I were among the crowd of 71st Street kids who were dropped off at Parkview Point by our mothers or older siblings for another spirited weekend of loud music, talk of adolescent girls, walks to the beach, and muddy football fields.
   Good times
   Neither of us could have imagined the other not being in the other's pocket.
   Darren leaving this world is just plain odd, first…
   Then impossible.
   The richness of our circle…
   It's like a pendant has been removed
   Adam and Sean and Bobby and Garret and Steven and John and Bruce…
   And myself
   Darren was well thought of
   Respected and much-loved

The COVID pandemic disallowed travel to his funeral
   Truthfully, I don't think there's one amongst us who could recite Kaddish without stumbling through a prayerbook
   So what counts, to be so bold
   Would be to declare our initial feelings unfolding at news of his death
   For myself
   Upon learning that our dear friend had passed
   I did not have a visual memory

But an aural recognition
I could clearly recall the quality and character of his voice
And then I surmised
How he had been an uncommonly serious person
How he was incapable of pretense
And indeed…
He had a way of saying things
As was shared by Sean Edelson on the day of Darren's passing:
"He was a thoughtful person"
Yes, in both senses of the word…
Thoughtful: naturally considerate
And…
Thoughtful: instantly pensive
I can remember his step
Funny…
Once in a while
When being introduced
Darren would say dismissively of himself
"I'm the cute one!"
He was a beautiful boy and a lovely man

The last time I saw Darren was about ten years ago
   I told him I thought he'd missed his true calling
   That he was too honest to fool people on Wall Street
   And that becoming manager of Colorado construction sites
   Couldn't do it for him, either
   (Though he very much liked this position)

Sitting on my beat-up sofa
I told him he was a true "people person"
And that I could see him leading a Reformed Jewish congregation
   As I thought and knew he truly cared
   He looked up at me like he was given to do
   And said, "David, that's not gonna happen in this life or in the next!"
   We both laughed

Darren Linksman fit into his name, I say
   He didn't have to be anyone else
   And he never was
   Mother and father Linksman gave him an intellectual foundation
   That could have accomplished anything
   But like the rest of us
   He wanted to watch television
   Algebra could wait!
   "Nanu-nanu!"
   And with two cuties around like sister Missy and young Darren
   Who do you think got their way?
   Please ... Mom!

Linksman didn't suffer fools
   And he was a man who asked a good question

And he wouldn't go see the last Clint Eastwood flick, *El Torino*
Because Clint's character dies in the end

We loved him
He was a sweetheart, he was…
He was not a dancer
He was not a singer
He loved the Avanti motorcar
But more the MGB…
Like little dudes should

Let's gather next year
Tell stories around his headstone
Read some poetry
Howl at the moon like we mean it
And let's light yahrzeit candles
And share thoughts and memories of our friend
Who died on the 29th of November
Darren Linksman
A prince
And a prince three times

—Maiche Lev

Flip-Flops

If you don't know…
Life is better with a pair of flip-flops on
Improves your attitude
Skippin' along
The old, thin, cheap kind
Available at the five-and-dime
For 89 cents

ONE-SIDED THOUGHT ON MODERN-DAY TEEN REBELLION

We all try to do a good job raising our kids
But there's always a point of vulnerability when they reach adolescence
Of course, they all sit in groups
Pushing each other to profess a hatred for their families
They all smoke powerful dope
They all go to parties where mom and dad aren't home
They've seen it hundreds of times on the TV
How to take a shot of whisky
Daddy's bar is open
Boyfriend's gone to the store for more JD
Some, more than others, have spent hours upon hours masturbating with hamster pornography
And suddenly your daughter is wasted drunk in a room with a linebacker from the football squad
She's real woozy thinking there's something kind and loving and sweet's about to happen
It ends with blood running down her leg
And vomit everywhere
He also manages to impregnate the lass before he's done
(There are over 1.4-million abortions in the United States every year)
She doesn't cry rape
She keeps it together to Über to her best friend's house

She doesn't want to talk
Tries to sleep it off
She and her friend embrace and weep together
Monday morning in school she gets looks and whispers
Tuesday, half the school is making cat calls
All the respect she'd naturally accrued through the years
Suddenly, entirely gone
That's where suicidal rage implements itself
And all daddy had to do in the weeks prior was scoff his usual scoff
And mom has been too severe to confide in for years
God forbid this ever be your family's plight
But it happens in both private and public schools everywhere

The parent must have a plan
For the child is just that…
An adolescent is yesterday's twelve-year-old…
A child
Kids want to feel grown up
I visited my big sister in Pennsylvania one year when I was in high school
And then in New York a few years later as a young man
And it was great
Don't hold up your standards
The greater the pressure, the greater the resistance
To punish
What makes it worse?

Don't know which God a parent can pray to these days
The linebacker is *real*
So is this new crystal-laden dope and the shot glass
Let's get these little bitches fucked up
And through all these initiations
The girls always gossip
And the boys always talk
Behind that door
The more awful her crying out
The more he thought he was doing something right
Did she run to the road…?
God forbid
Lord protect my child

I ♥ ...

I'm just a love machine…

Some say love, it is a river…

Wo-oh-oh-ohh, ohh, sweet love

Love … love will keep us together

Ran out 'f love

Love will find a way

Madly in love

I fell deeply in love with you the moment we met…

Broken love, out on the highway

Love in an elevator

Lovesick

I hate myself for loving you

Because the night belongs to lovers

Long distance love affairs never work…

I'd love to turn you on…

All's fair in love and war

Amor, ahava, amour, liebe, люблю…

The hands of love

My love does it good

If y' find someone who gives you all of her love…

Take it to your heart and don't let it stray

I know you love me, Maiche…

If only…

Hello love…

We hurt the ones we love the most

New love

An all-consuming love
I love that song…
What about love?
Don't you want someone to care about you?
I love that show
And in the end the love you make
   is equal to the love you take…
I love that movie
I love that band
Feel like makin' love
Try a little love
The Love Boat…
(soon will be dah dah dah dee dah dah…)
Love?
Lord above… now you're tryin' to trick me in love
I'm so sick of those who feel they've got a monopoly on love
The ways of love
Lookin' for love in all the wrong places
There was a moment when I really loved her…
Then one day the feeling just died
To search for love: That ain't no more than vanity
I love chopped liver
I love chopped liver on melba toast
What's not to love in a world with so much to hate?
To live for love
To die for love
Money can't buy you love

Endless love, my endless love
My lessons at love's pain and heartache school
Short people got nobody to love…
The road to love is littered by the bones of other ones…
Who by the magic of the moment were mysteriously undone[7]
Puppy love
I think I love you!
(Hi, Debbie)
I love the '77 MGB "Soft Nose" in Costello green
Your love doesn't haunt me like it did before
You've got a face that yearns for love
Everybody knows that love's the finest thing around[8]
I love my grandmother
I love my Birkenstocks
I love my cat
I love my dog
I love my blue budgie
The things she tolerates from my African Gray!
I love to spend Shabbat with the Orthodox
I love it when my apartment is clean
I'm in love with a black woman … and I'm so glad
There's a thin line between love and hate
I live the life I love and I love the life I live
What you won't do, you'll do for love

---

7 Gordon Lightfoot, "Race Amongst the Ruins," *Summertime Dream,* Reprise Records, 1976
8 Taylor, James, "Carolina in my Mind," *James Taylor,* Apple Records, 1968

GRITTY CORSAGE

Left with an island that's four feet underwater
Which, by the way
Is no island at all...
All the children's teeth are rotting
From mixing Mountain Dew with grain alcohol
All the party people
Yeah...
Big party goin' on
Dance floor
Its own religion
The house mother keeps showin' me pictures
Of my brothers hangin' off each tit
It's only the silent stranger you could call compassionate
And they break into *Auld Lang Syne*
1 – 2 – 3 – 4
Jesus *walks* in...
The female Jesus
The saint of whatcomesnext
She's in her boots and motorcycle jacket
Sits next to me on the gritty floor
And she says to me this:

You will suffer no deed
No deed will press
The sun
The salt

142 — Maiche Lev

The winds
The sand
Waves like cymbals crashing on rocks
Out in the distance

She cups my face and says:

Man must be born again for reasons only the simplest

You need a ride?
Let's get out of here

Another One

At some times in your life
Your measure as a man
Is stood by how well you can apologize
Describing the feelings
From a humbled will

More Later

Beware of lightning strikes
Period!
You are who your friends are
But, your honor…
What's powerful is also dangerous
It's too late when you finally see
You can't tame a lion
Try as you may
No one loves you like your mother
Hope springs eternal
We hurt the ones we love the most
You can never go home
Ya can't roller-skate in a buffalo roam
Some never learn
Y' can't teach an old dog a new trick
Dog years or people years?
There's more than one way to fix stuttering
Probably more than one way to inherit it, too
Y' got no reason to be a star if y' don't want your
    picture taken
Little Richard said that
Y' can't fix stupid
But y' can feed it endless distraction
If y' don't stand for something you'll fall for anything
Yup

Nothing matters ... and what if it did?
Mark Twain?
The Lord hates a coward
There stands I, at the junior high school dance
A bird with no feet sleeps in the wind
A line from a poem I read as a kid
If you can't beat 'em, join 'em
Famous last words
All for one and one for all
I knew this was a bad idea
There's nothing wrong with her a hundred dollars won't fix
It will destroy your family; your happy home is gone
The devil's been busy in your backyard
I hear you knockin' but you can't come in
Truth be told, you make up the bed you sleep in
Conscience can sometimes be a pest

He Would Know…

Life is cheap where there is excessive violence
Extreme trespass leads to feelings of worthlessness
The virtues of purity are lost in poverty
Think about that

A herd is known to run in circles
Impulsiveness from pridefulness
Leads to wanting to tear your teeth out
Wanting to crawl out of your own skin

Impatience…
Perturbation…
Hurtfulness…
Snap judgements and intolerance are the same malignancy

Cruelty is a heavy, irresistible chord progression
A wicked drumroll
From the militancy of adolescence

Nobody laughs when somebody's crying, children
If you can speak kindness
You will be thought of as merciful and wise
To be wise is to reveal righteous measure
And that is important

Lay yourself down when you're out in the rain
'Cause lightning will kill you

Buckles, Ties, Loops, Rings, Wraps, and Clasps, Baby! — 149

BRUCE JENNER

Bruce Jenner had his need for attention
Piqued on Oprah Winfrey's couch
And Ellen DeGeneris's love seat
And a little later
He became she…
Kylie Jenner

All this…
Under the same light of salvation we all stand…
Attention
America's decathlon champion
You always have to be careful
Somewhat apologetic
With the LGBTQ community

I am not one who dreams of hurting anyone
But if my son or daughter could do nothing
But dilly-dally their born composition away
It's well enough that I wish you…
But I will see you no more

Heartbreaker

People

I find people to be smart and surprisingly bright
But people sometimes hear what they want to hear
And they'll assassinate your character in spells of laughter,
   if you let them.
To drive a butcher's knife between your radius and ulna
Outstretched in greeting
For any such rumormonger
Would serve well to properly psychologically scar that person
So smart and surprisingly bright…

TRUMP

Did he once in four years show any sign of genuine emotion?
Any true feelings…?
No
Just every once in a while
A dry, doltish, inappropriate joke
De Niro's Capone
The dumb exalt him
So wrapped up in the American flag
With their Q-Anon Dixie Cups
No job
No money
No education
But a big gun to keep clean
Did he push for or even mention a twelve-dollar minimum wage?
No
What he really did was deal sleight-of-hand racism
To the foaming rabid
And how do you feel about five people being killed in our capitol building?
It would have been disgusting enough if they'd just come in and trashed the place…
But five people dead!?

Trump exploited the dumb
And the dumb buy all this unhinged conspiracy horseshit

"Got my ammo at the gun show in Seymour last month"
Seventy-million Republicans stood next to him to vote for
   four more years
Where would you rather be than at a Trump rally?
Rather be on another continent learning my ABCs

Hypermasculine Horseshit Falls

Guns
Gunsandsex
Gunsandsexandmoney
Gunsandsexandmoneyandnews
Gunsandsexandmoneyandnewsandtalk
Gunsandsexandmoneyandnewsandtalkandsports
Gunsandsexandmoneyandnewsandtalkandsportsandlaughs
AndspeedandfightsandmorefightsandexplosionsandbitchinessandrichesandbandsandrapandarmiesonthemarchandBobRoss
Hey, he taught me how to paint…!

There You Go

I just went for cigarettes at 7-11
Some young Black dudes there
All the look…
I said to the one near me
"Hey, your pants are falling down.
We can see your underwear and everything."
He didn't say much, 'cept for something under his breath
And I paid and left

Knowing they'd pursue
I walked home on the side street
And they did
About four minutes later
In their mom's lowered maroon Toyota
   with the tinted-windows

I turned around
Reversed my direction
And walked toward them in the middle of the street
Right at their headlights
A door opened as they slowly passed
The car stopped
And one of 'em popped his head out saying,
   "Hey, come here"

I kept walking past them
It ended there
But right now I could be dead

The dignity of King
Malcolm X's drive
Bob Marley and the Wailers' universal victory
Does it even exist today?

Well, I loves the 54, too

Spike Lee introduced the word "gentrification"
To the unfortunate world of blight and ghetto
Everybody seems to be a few steps away from killing
    one another…
And this is my little 7–11 story

In their car right now they're saying
"Let's go back and get that fuckin' white-ass bitch!"
It's a wonderful world
Pull up your trousers
Read a book
Abandon!

I'D LIKE TO...

I'd like to put a hole in the bottom of two metal cans
Tie up a string
Make a telephone

I'd like to build a soapbox racer
Drive all the way to work
Miles from my home

I'd like to get a marker
And draw a beard on my face
Darker and darker
Like daddy's

I'd like to get my tennis racquet out
And play a mean guitar
With the radio loud...

I'd like to fly off the roof in a cape I've pinned 'neath my chin
I am I am I am Superman
And I can do anything!

I'd like to build a lemonade stand
And pour from a pitcher into Dixie cups
How much should we get for a cupful?
I dunno...
I haven't given it a thought...

Me and my sisters gonna put on a Broadway show in the living room
We put a television on top of the car the night they say there was a man on the moon

I'm gonna sleep in my treehouse!
I'm gonna throw rocks at a wasp's nest
I'm gonna put a butter knife in the electrical outlet
I'm gonna holler, "Harr, mateys!"
Captain of the pirates
I'm gonna steal some gum with Joey at the corner store
I'm gonna build forts on Saturday morning
And crawl around on my hands and knees

I'm gonna build a space ship out of boxes
Keep a flashlight for when we pass the last star
Out there
In galaxies beyond…
Planets…
Moons…
The asteroid belt…
Whatever…

I'm gonna ride my dog like he was a horse

I'm gonna ride my bike
Build a ramp
Skid out on the hill on the golf course

Oh, let's wash Doctor Renfield's car again

I'd like to go to Disney World again
20,000 Leagues Under the Sea
Country Bear Jamboree
Pirates of the Caribbean ... the cannonballs!
Space Mountain
If only it didn't take so long to get there!

I know...
Let's go fishin'!

No...
Let's go to the Bowl-o-Mat
Did you get your allowance?

www.ingramcontent.com/pod-product-compliance
Lightning Source LLC
Chambersburg PA
CBHW031147160426
43193CB00008B/281